Food From Mars

by Marlene Thornton

Nothing in this book is to be reproduced without author's permission. Unless you are cooking it. ☺

Marlene Thornton made up all the recipes that are included.

Published in August of 2014

I have been all over the western side of Canada, and the USA. The culinary art changes as you pass from the East to the west of Canada. It also does in the USA.

Starting in Mactaquac New Brunswick. The harsh climate changes produces mostly root vegetables. Then, there are cows, and a few pigs. Turkeys do well in this climate for the summer in the deep woods. You will also find chickens.

Where there are cows, there is milk. Also New Brunswick has cheese, and butter from the cows. Apples grow very well so there is abundance in the summer.

Fredericton is in a circle of a hundred miles of woods. It is straight in the middle. Honeybees do well so there is plenty of that. Because Fredericton is in the woods, there are plenty of wild animals. Moose grow there, and deer's, rabbits, and bears. There is plenty of the culinary art world there.

Maple syrup is made from sap from the trees. So there is lots of sugar. Apples grow in many kinds, and berries. Potatoes are a main staple. The man who invented different types of apples came from there. He was my grandfather. Fredericton went into starvation mode at one point. It was my grandfather taught them how to use the seed. How to dry the seed out, and have gardens for next year.

The food is different than other parts of Canada. People in Fredericton usually do not get away from it. So there food is what the people made up. In past times, they did not have cook books. If they had one, it was one or two from the community. People out in the country like Mactaquac did not get to town much. I was one of them, and had to make up the food. If I wanted Pizza, I had to make it up myself.

We did not have the internet in the 70's. I would need to start from making the bottom to the top. I made what I thought was chili con carne. Living in the wild gave great culinary art skills. The food was based on meat, potatoes, and vegetables for the most part. Baked beans on Saturday, and beef on Sunday.

When you get into the town of Fredericton, the food is a bit different. It is twenty-eight miles from Mactaquac. There are restaurants of a few different cultures. Chinese. Italian, and so forth. Living in the woods, I did not taste Chinese food before. I tried it in the 1980's, and real pizza in town. We usually made them in Mactaqauc. A lot of people there put wieners on their pizza. I was cooking at the age of seven.

Once you get up into Edmonstun, and Montreal the food changes a bit. They eat beans with their breakfast in a little bowl. It consists of normal eggs, and bacon. It is rather a good combination, I thought.

Alberta eats a lot of roast beef, and beef in general. This is where I learned how to cook a proper steak. Also, they have the best clam chowder in the world. I was out to find the best. I worked on my own clam chowder recipe. I loved clam chowder, but most I had was not good. There was only one time I ever got good clam chowder. I have added my recipe in the book.

I went to college in Edmonton Alberta for three years. One year of it was in professional cooking. I graduated with an 89%. Here I met my teacher Iron Chef George. I wanted to learn new food as I only knew food from Mactaquac.

There were many different courses. One was meat cutting, and meat in general. Iron chef George taught me how to know what to cook meat in. We held science labs boiling different meat in different liquids. My team boiled beef in milk. Another team would boil it in orange juice. Ours came out the softest. The milk broke down the fibers in the meat. The orange juice made it tough. If we boiled fish in the juice, it was good. Fish does not have strong fibers like a cow.

We also took a course in sauces. We learned all the mother sauces. How a hollandaise is turned into a béarnaise. Then how to fix the mother sauces to make another. From learning all the sauces, I learned how to make fruit dips.

There was a course in five course meals. We would need to prepare the meal. Then, serve it to Iron Chef George before time was up. I learned a lot how to prepare garnishes in this course. Iron Chef George was pleased with my garnishes I made up. I would use orange cups for fruit sauces. This is where I learned all garnishes must be edible.

You can coat grapes with sugar that has a few drops of cherry juice in it. First you dip the grape into milk. After putting into the cherry sugar, let them dry. They are good for cake decorations or in a fruit salad. The cherry sugar is great on top of sugar cookies also.

We had a course in baking. Iron chef told the whole class I probably would not do well. He said people that come from Mactaquac did not know how to bake. We only knew how to make soups. I proved him wrong, and kept my 89% mark. I learned how to make puff pastry. It grew like I have never seen anything grow before. It took three days working with the pastry, and kneading it with butter. After I was done, one bowl became a 24-foot table's length. I ran out of ideas using it. I made little Danish pastries, that when done where huge. I got very good marks, and he admired me for my skills. This is the course I learned how to pipe things into the puff pastry after done. You put the cream into a piping bag, and put it in one end.

You will find the context at the end of the book.

Easy ways of fixing things around the house

If you get hot peppers on your skin, use milk to take away the burning.

Use lemon juice, and salt on your boards. Do this after cutting chicken or pork to disinfect.

Use brown paper bags to grease baking pans.

Pour comet on a cloth will take off grim. Also, it will work on the fridge or anything to take discolor away.

Put tinfoil under, and above your baking sheet. Your baking won't burn.

Drink one of those lemon plastic yellow lemons. A little throughout the day. It will stop a sore throat, flu, asthma, and can stop certain cancers. Also it will stop a bad cough.

Lettuce in stainless steel in the fridge lasts longer or in tin foil.

Put tin foil on all your baking pans before adding the food. It saves your pans.

Greek Pockets

Your favorite piecrust not baked
Greek feta cheese with herbs - 1 pound
Minced olives any kind - 6
Romano Cheese - 1 container
Pepper- to taste
Basil- just a bit
Lemon juice - a half of one

Method

Mix all of the ingredients, but pie crust together. Roll the pie crust out between two plastic bags. Cut with a large round glass, and put some filling in. Make sure it isn't too full as you must make into a half circle. Just roll one end over to the other. Bake at 375F until done.

Homemade Sausage's

Veal - One-pound ground
Pork - One-pound ground
Fennel - just a tad
Onion spice - just a tad
Pepper - just a tad
Garlic - 2 teaspoons minced
Caraway - just a tad
Hot pepper - only if you want, and just a tad
Cheese - marble cheese one cup shredded

Method

Mix everything together, and roll about a quarter of a cup in some saran wrap. Make it the size you want your sausages. Boil these in the saran wrap in hot boiling water for ten minutes.

After done, take the saran wrap off. Fry until brown and serve.

Greek Sukiyaki

Chicken or pork - 2 pounds boneless, large cubes raw
Basil - two tablespoons
Lemon juice - 1/4 cup
Sunflower oil- ¾'s cup
Rice - two cups cooked
Tomato paste - two tablespoons
Louisiana spice - to taste
Pepper - to taste
Garlic - one clove
Onion salt - one teaspoon
Pita shells

Method

Cube the chicken or pork into large chunks. Marinate in the next three ingredients for at least 2 hours. In the meantime make the rice. Put the small wooden skewers in cold water.

Fry the rice, and the rest of ingredients in a frying pan. Now, put the chicken on the skewers, and grill until brown. Put some rice on each pita shell, and then the chicken off the skewer. Wrap like a gyro or donair, and wrap in tin foil, then serve.

P.S. You will notice that the marinate almost cooks the meat while it is raw.

Homemade Pita or Tortilla Shells

Flour - 3 cups
Baking powder - 2 teaspoons
Salt - ¾'s of a teaspoon
Warm water - 1 cup

Method

Stir together the first three ingredients. Gradually stir in the water, and make sure it is crumbly dough at first. Now, take the dough out into your hands, and make into a ball.

Knead on board until smooth. Divide into 10 or so pieces, and shape into a ball. Put plastic wrap over them, and let rest for fifteen minutes.

Now flatten one ball into a patty on a floured board. Roll from center to edges, and roll very thin. Turn it often as you are doing this. Thinner is better. Fry each in a dry frying pan at 375F. Almost instantly, tiny bubbles should appear. Turn the tortilla shell, and place the spatula on top of it.

Wrap the cooked ones in plastic, and place in a towel. You can wrap these in foil when cool, and freeze. Or serve when they are done steaming in towel.

You can cut these into triangles, and deep-fry them. Or use them for pita sandwiches or sukiyaki.

Donair Pizza

Bread recipe
Hamburger - 2 pounds
Seasoning salt - lots to sprinkle around the hamburger
Donair sauce - one bottle or container. You can find this at your local grocery store. If not I will add a recipe or an alternative next.
Lettuce - ½ of a head diced small
Onion - one medium red or white small diced
Tomatoes - 3 or 4 small dice, and fresh

Method

Take your angel food cake pan, and place the entire hamburger around it. Sprinkle a lot of seasoning salt all over the outside of it. Bake in a 375F oven until done.

Take some of the raw pizza dough as much as you desire. Flour a board, and roll the dough out. Use a plastic bag under, and flour it. Then, use a plastic bag over top.

Then, you can roll. This pizza is better with a thicker crust. Put your dough now on your buttered pizza pan. Poke holes in the bottom of it. Bake it in a 375F oven until very lightly brown. If it starts to rise while cooking, take a fork and poke it. When done, take out.

Slice the donair meat you made. Make it around 1 and ¼ inches each, and thin. Add as much as you want of the donair sauce first on the baked dough.

Place the thin slices of donair meat all over the pizza. Mix the small-diced tomatoes, small-diced lettuce, and onions. Add this over the meat. Serve

Tzatziki Sauce

Alternative for donair sauce, and it is Greek.

French vanilla yogurt - one cup
Sour cream - ½ of a cup
Cucumber - ¼ of a cup seeds taken out
Dill - enough to flavor to your liking
Lemon juice - one teaspoon

Method

Place everything in a mixer, and don't mix for
very long.

Clam Chowder

Celery - 3 pieces chopped along with the center
Bacon - one pound diced raw
Onion - 1 large diced small
Garlic - two bulbs diced small
Half & half - 1 quart
Whipping Cream - 1 quart get a lot to cover this
Mushroom soup - 1 can
Pepper - to taste
Clams - one large can
Lemon juice - 3 tablespoons
Potatoes - 4 cups raw, and cut into small chunks
Dill - 1½ teaspoons

Method

Dice the bacon, celery, onion small, and fry. Do not fry the mixture crisp just until the onions are transparent.

Add the milks, spices, water, clam juice, and mushroom soup. Simmer on low for a couple hours. Add the clams the last ten minutes of cooking. This is a thick clam chowder.

P.S. You can use any sort of fish you desire. It only takes fish up to 15 minutes to cook in the broth. So do not add the fish until last.

Spaghetti Sauce

Hamburger - one pound fried
Onions - one diced
Garlic - one whole clove
Red pepper - one diced
Green pepper - one diced
Stewed tomatoes - One large can
Tomato paste - one can
Basil - to taste
Oregano - a dash
Pepper - a dash
Soy sauce - ¼ cup
Seasoning salt - to taste
Mushrooms - ½ of a pound

Method

Fry the hamburger, onions, and peppers, and garlic.
Add everything else, and simmer on low for a half
hour. You can use pepperoni or ground sausage in
the hamburgers place.

Spinach and Ham Lasagna

Spinach - 2 large bags cook in boiling water, and drain
Ham - one pound sliced thin, and small pieces
Onions - one large minced
Seasoning salt - to your own taste
Mozzarella cheese - shredded, and use as much as you
desire
Cottage cheese - one large container
Garlic - one clove
Pepper - a dash
Seasoning salt - sparingly

Method

Cook noodles. Put a layer of ham, spinach, onions, cheeses,
spices then noodles. Keep doing this until done.

Make sure the last layer is noodle. Top with mozzarella
cheese. Bake at 375F until done

Cinnamon Toast

White sugar - One cup
Cinnamon - 2 tablespoons
Icing sugar - ¼ cups

Method

Mix it altogether. Butter toast, and put a tablespoon or so on.

Classified Chicken

Chicken pieces - one whole chicken
Onion - one sliced
Garlic - four minced
Thyme - enough to coat all chicken in bowl
Salt - a dash
Pepper - a dash
Lemon juice - to rub the chicken
Save the liquids from the chicken

Method

Clean chicken pieces, and rub with lemon juice. Add the
chicken, onion, and garlic to bowl. Coat pieces with thyme,
add salt, and pepper. Fry until brown then add the liquid
left from chicken. Cover, and simmer until done.

Shepherd's Pie

Ground beef - 2 pounds
Seasoning salt - 1 teaspoon
Garlic salt - 2 teaspoon
Onion - one medium minced
Tomato Paste - 2 cans
Corn - 3 cups
Mashed potatoes - enough to cover the top
Butter - 8 tables spoons

Method

Fry the beef with the onion, and tomato paste in a frying
pan. Add the seasoning salt, and garlic. Put all of this into a
large pan. Put the cooked corn on top of this. Top with
mashed potatoes, and dot the butter on top. Bake until
golden brown on 375F

P.S. You can top it also with shredded cheese of any kind if
you desire. Or add the cheese into the mashed potatoes.

Meat Pie

Pie crust for top, and bottom.
Stew of any kind

Method

Fill an unbaked pie crust with stew, and cover with the other shell. Poke a couple fork holes in the middle on top. Bake at 375F until golden brown. Great way to use leftover stew.

Chicken Pot Pie

Chicken stew; add ½ cup of cream to the top. Do this before adding the top shell.

Home Made Bread

Water - 6 cups of Luke warm
Fast rising yeast - 3 tablespoons
White sugar - 3 tablespoons
White flour enough to keep adding to form a soft ball.
It would be impossible to tell you the amount just buy a
rather large one.
Oil - a bit to add almost at the end

Method

Add the yeast to the warm water. Make sure the water is
not to hot or not to cold. Also, add the sugar, and do not stir
this. Let it set until it rises up, and then start adding floor.
Just add a couple cups at a time.

Stir and then add more. When it gets too heavy to stir, add
it to a floured board. Kneed the bread, and keep flouring
your board. It shouldn't be over floured or to little just
right.

Now, form it into a ball with your hands. Use all of it the
same time, and now add some oil all over it. When it feels
right, add it to a large oiled bowl. Cover this in a nice warm
place until it rises. It should rise high, and then bang it
down.

Use your hands to do this, and let it rise one more time.
Now, don't bang it down, but make your bread, buns, or
whatever. Cover with some cloth, and let rise one more
time. Bake in a 375F oven until brown.

When nicely brown, lay on a cloth. Sprinkle water or butter
on top, and sides. Cover with another cloth, and let set to
steam. P.S. You can use this for pizza dough, cinnamon
buns, or add shredded cheese.

Sandwiches

Tuna on toast

Tuna - Drain one or two cans
White mayonnaise - not a lot add a little at a time
You will know what you like, but it should not be runny.
White sugar - 1 1/2 teaspoons
White toast - Hot and buttered

Method

Mix all together except the bread. Add a fair amount on.
Some salt, and pepper tastes good as well.

Tuna on Bread

Tuna - 2 cans drained
Onion - 1 ½ tablespoons
Celery - 3 tablespoons small minced
Dill pickles – 2 small minced
White sugar - 1 tablespoon
White mayonnaise - add a little at a time until to your liking

Method

Butter both sides on untoasted bread, and add a fair
amount. Salt and pepper if you like.

Egg and Cheese

Egg - 1
Cheese - one cheese slice
English Muffin - 1

Method

Fry the egg on one side. Add the cheese once the egg has sit to the right stage. You will know the way you like your egg. Once you add the cheese, take it off the burner. Keep the pan covered. Toast and butter the English muffin.

Add the egg onto the muffin, and serve.

Grilled Cheese Egg in the Hole

White bread - 2 pieces
Cheddar cheese slices - 2 pieces
Butter
Egg - 1
Cajun spice - a touch for on top

Method

Put the cheese on the bread. Put the top piece of bread on top. Take a circle out of the middle all the way through. Put a fair amount of butter on all sides of the bread on the outside.

Put this in a frying pan on medium heat 325 degrees. Let both sides get a bit brown. Then, add the egg into the hole, and a touch of Cajun spice on top.

Let it fry for a moment then turn. You want the middle of the egg still runny. It is not a sandwich to eat with your fingers.

I eat mine with ketchup on the side.

P.S.

You can make round balls with the bread from the middle. Put butter on them, and fry to make cheese balls.

Red Spaghetti Sauce on Vermicelli

Hamburger - 4 pounds
Fresh Garlic - 2 cloves crushed
Seasoning salt - 1 or so tablespoons
Garlic spice - 1 or so tablespoons
Chives - 3 tablespoons
Oregano - 1 tablespoon
Spanish white onion - 1/2 of one large
Green pepper - 1
Tomatoes - 1 large can already chopped
Hunts thick tomato sauce - 1 large can
Tomato paste - 1 small can
Vermicelli - 2 round circles the size of a golf ball
Oil - as the recipe requires

Method

Fry the hamburger, and spices until almost done. Add the large chopped onion, and green peppers. Fry until onions are almost cooked. Add everything else, and simmer for a half hour.

Boil a large pot of water, and some salt. Also, add a bit of oil to this. Get the water boiling really well, and then you can add the vermicelli. Take one bunch of it, and cut it in half while adding to the water. Then add the next, and use a fork to separate. Vermicelli cooks really fast.

Strain the vermicelli in a colander, and then add a bit of oil or butter. Shake the pasta to get the oil onto it. Now, you can put some onto a plate, and put the sauce on top. I do not cook with salt much. I find this sauce to have enough natural salt. We usually add salt or pepper after anyhow.

Yorkshire Pudding
The method is very important in this recipe.

White milk - 8 oz. cup
Eggs - 3 large
Flour - 1½ cups
Butter - 12 teaspoons

Method

When first starting the roast beef, take the first two ingredients out of fridge. Most beef roasts cook in two hours or a half. Leave the first two ingredients on the counter until roast is cooked. .

It is important that both are at room temperature. Get a muffin tin that holds twelve muffins. Place one teaspoon of butter in each muffin tin. Place the muffin tin into the oven on 375 degrees.

In the meantime make the Yorkshire pudding. Place the flour into a large bowl. With a fork whisk in the three eggs. Don't beat too much it should be lumpy. Add quarter of the milk at a time, and mix each time. Not too much at a time.

Take the muffin tin out of the oven, and place ¾ ways up of Yorkshire pudding into each tin. Place in the oven, and don't open the oven while cooking. It is a good idea to have a light in the oven so you can turn it on while baking. They are done when the tops are puffy, and light brown.

They are good opened up at the top, and beef put in. Then, the gravy you make from the beef drippings.

Barbecue Porcupines

Hamburger - 2 pounds raw
Instant rice - ½ cups
Onion - ½ cup chopped fine
Seasoning salt to your liking
Garlic salt or bulbs - chopped fine, and add enough to your liking
Water - ½ cup

Method

Mix everything together, and put on a pan with tin foil. Make the balls to around one inch.

Sauce

Ketchup 1 cup
Soy sauce 5 tablespoons
seasoning salt to your liking
Garlic salt or minced garlic to your liking
Brown sugar ½ cup

Method

Mix everything together, and place on top of the meatballs. Bake in a 375-degree oven until done. Usually it takes 45 minutes. Half ways through cooking drain some of the liquid off the meatballs.

I like to serve these with mashed potatoes, and buttered baby carrots

Chili

Hamburger - 2 pounds
Onion - 1/2 of a cup
Tomatoes - 1 large cannot drained crushed
Kidney beans - 1 large cannot drained
Tomato soup - 1 can
Tomato paste - 1 can
Garlic - 1 tablespoon minced
Garlic powder - to taste
Seasoning salt - to taste
Mushrooms - 2 cups fresh sliced
Chili powder - I go by taste as some chili powder is hotter than others. Add a little then you can add more after.
Green pepper - 1 chopped and no seeds
Red pepper - 1 chopped and no seeds
Honey - 1/4 cup you can use brown sugar

Method

Fry the hamburger until almost done, and add onions. Fry a bit more then add everything else. Simmer on a low temperature for an hour or so.

It goes good with potato salad. There are times I don't add the green, and red pepper. It still is good.

Country Fried Steak

Steak - 1 large cheap cut
Crackers - 1 sleeve finely crushed
White flour - 1 cup
Baking powder - 1 teaspoon
Red Pepper - 1 teaspoon
Black pepper - 1 teaspoon
Salt - 1 teaspoon
Eggs - 2 large
Milk - 3/4 of a cup

Method

In a food processor chop the steak until just chopped. You don't want it ground. Mix everything, but the milk. Now mix the eggs, and milk together. Make oval shapes from the beef. Dip it into the cracker, and flour mixture, then into the milk mixture, and back into the cracker mixture. Bake at 375 until golden brown. It is served with white gravy, but I do not like the white gravy. It is always eaten with mashed potatoes. They don't eat vegetables with it, but I do.

Deep Fried Turkey

Turkey Breast - 1 uncooked
Flour - 1 cup all purpose
Fajita spice - 1 tablespoon
Cajun Spice - 2 teaspoons
Oil - to fry in enough to deep fry 1 inch deep

Method

Add the spices to the flour. Slice the turkey into strips.
Get the oil hot. Dip the turkey into the flour, and fry
until golden brown. Don't overcook or the turkey will
get dry.

Tacos

Hamburger fried - 2 pounds
Taco seasoning - 2 packages
Water - 2 cups
Tomatoes - diced small
Lettuce - cut small
Onion - diced small
Salsa
Sour cream
Cheddar cheese - grated
Pita bread or taco shells

Method

Fry the hamburger until done. I think they call it mince in
England not sure. Add the taco seasoning, and water. Cook
until the water is gone. Warm the pita in a microwave for a
few seconds only. Add some of the beef mixture. Then add
the vegetables, salsa, and cheese on top. Roll up, and it is
ready.

Country Fried Chicken

Chicken Pieces - 6
White flour - 1 cup
Fine bread crumbs - 1 1/2
Seasoning salt - add a lot
Pepper - add a lot of that
dried minced garlic - add a lot

Method

Clean the chicken in water. Then mix everything together, and shake the chicken in it. Bake chicken for 45 minutes at 375F

Latke Potatoes

Potatoes - 5 peeled, and shredded
Onion - 1 medium diced small
Egg - 1
Flour - 3 tablespoons

Method

Put the potatoes through a food processor for just a second.
You want shreds not mush or large pieces. Put the potatoes
on a cloth, and make sure all the water is squeezed out of
them.

Add the potatoes, onion, egg, and flour to a bowl. Mix this
altogether. Add a fair amount, but not a lot of oil to a frying
pan. Make sure the pan is hot, Make like hamburger patties
from the potato mixture. Fry on one side until golden
brown. Turn, and allow the other side to brown. I like to
add a bit of seasoning salt on them while they fry.

Serve with sour cream

Sweet and Sour Sauce

Ketchup - 1 cup
Brown sugar - one cup
Pineapple - ½ cups drained, and crushed
Cherries - 10 crushed

Method

Mix now altogether, and warm this on the stove.

It is great on meatballs with some green pepper, carrots, and onions added. Then put on some white rice. Or you can use it for a dipping sauce.

White Wine Seafood Sauce

Onion - one large
One shallot - minced
Garlic – 1 bulb
Lemon juice - to your taste
Dill - 2 teaspoons
Olive oil - a small amount
White wine - ¼ cup
Salmon - 1 can drain
Crab - 1 can drained
Dijon mustard - 1 teaspoon
Shrimp - 1 pound fresh
A bottle of capers drained
Cream - 1 large container. You can use half an half or whipping cream
Angel Hair pasta - cooked

Method

Fry the first six ingredients. Allow this to simmer for a few moments, and then add the rest. Allow to simmer. You don't want to take long making this. Fish does not require a long cooking period. Thicken some water with cornstarch. Add enough to your liking of thickness, and stir. I would add a little at a time. Now it is ready to put on top of your pasta to eat.

P.S. You can use any sort of fish you like

Meat Rolls

Ground meat - 1 pound
Onion - one minced
A pinch of salt and pepper
Garlic - add to your taste
Seasoning salt - to your taste
Grated cheese - 1 cup
Egg roll wrappers
Egg - 1

Method

Fry first five ingredients until done. Mix the egg in a bowl
with a little bit of milk. Add a couple teaspoons on each
wrapper. Shred some fresh cheese on each of these. Egg
wash with your fingers. On all sides wrap it up. Put a few
into a deep fryer until done.

Italian Beef on a Bun

Beef roast - 2 pounds, and grind the meat in a cusinart
Garlic - 4 tbsp.
Onion - 1 large minced.
Seasoning salt - to taste
Pepper - a dash
Italian spice - to taste
Gardenia - ½ cup minced in blender
Long buns

Method

Put the raw meat into a pot with everything else. Season as you are simmering 1½ hours. Use the juice to dip the top of the bun. Add the beef then some gardenia, and then the top piece of bread.

German Stuffing for Turkey or Chicken

Onion - One large cut fine
Boxed stuffing – 1 country style or turkey flavor
Mashed potatoes - 5 pounds
Eggs - 2
Pepper - a dash
Seasoning salt - to taste
Garlic powder - to taste
Sage - 2 tablespoons or to taste
Savory - 2 teaspoons or to taste
Rosemary - 2 tablespoons grounded

Method

Mix altogether, and stuff the bird.

Scalloped Potatoes

Potatoes - as many as you need for your pan
Milk enough to cover the potatoes
Garlic - to taste
Salt and Pepper - to taste
Flour - ¾ cup, and maybe some more
Onion - 1 large
Butter - ¼ cup

Peel, and thinly slice enough potatoes to go in your pan. Make sure they are cut in ¼ inch thick circles. Cut a large onion up. Add some garlic salt, and pepper.

Add ¾ cup of flour, and you can add shredded cheese if you like. Top it up with milk to the top of the dish. Make sure everything is covered. Add the butter in chunks

Bake on 375F until half cooked. You might need be take it out, and add more flour. It is done when the top is getting golden. Make sure the potatoes are tender.

P.S. You can, also, add some chopped cooked ham to it if you like in the beginning.

Piggy's in a Blanket

Shortening - 1 cup
Flour - 3 cups
Baking powder - 3 heaping tablespoons
Milk - ¼ cup or less
Miracle whip - ¼ cup

Method

Use a fork to blend shortening, and flour. Don't stir too much or it will get over worked. Add the baking powder, and baking soda.

Now add enough milk to make into dough. Add the quarter cup of miracle whip, and whisk.

Put a plastic bag on to your table, and add a little flour all over the bag. Spread the dough out into a square. Cut little squares out, and add a 1/2 wiener in each. Wrap up around the dough. Put on a greased baking pan, and bake until they are brown. Bake at 350 degree's

French Toast

Bread - 2
Eggs - 2 large
Milk - ¼ cup
Oil - 2 tablespoons

Method

Put the eggs in a bowl, and add the milk. Get a frying pan very hot, and add 2 tablespoons of oil. Dip each side into the egg mixture. Fry on both sides until nice, and brown.

When done, put two on a plate. Add a bit of butter on each. In a cup add lots of cinnamon to some icing sugar. You can use this on top with some pancake syrup.

Meat Loaf Delight

Hamburg - 2 Pounds
Eggs - 1
Cracker crumbs or bread crumbs - ½ cups
Oatmeal - ½ cups
Garlic - minced to taste
Seasoning salt - to taste to
Pepper - to taste
Onion - one large diced small
 Ketchup - 1 ½ cups
Brown sugar - ½ cup

Method

Mix all the ingredients together except the last two. Put it all in a bread pan. On top add the ketchup, and sugar. Bake at 400F until brown on top.

Serve with mashed potatoes, and your favorite vegetable. It also goes very good with white rice, and butter on it.

Egg in the Hole

Egg - 1
Bread - 1 piece
Seasoning salt - to taste
Butter to fry in

Method

Take the middle out of the bread. Heat the pan with the grease in it. Add the bread, and cook on both sides. Then put the egg in the middle, and season it. Fry until egg is the way you like it.

P.S. You can put cheese on top, and melt it if you like.

Marinated Mushrooms

Fresh mushrooms - 1 1/2 pounds
Olive oil - 3/4 cups
Wine vinegar - 1/3 cup
Lemon juice - 3 tablespoons
Chopped chives - 4 tsps.
Chopped parsley - 1/4 cup
 Tarragon - 1 1/2 tsps.
Salt - 1 1/2 tsps.
Ground black pepper - 1 1/2 tsps.
Honey - 2 tsps.

Method

Wipe mushrooms with a damp cloth, and set aside.
Mix all ingredients well except the mushrooms. Pour
everything all over the mushrooms. Cover and chill
for several hours. Overnight is best. Stir occasionally.

Honey Mustard Sauce

Plain Mustard - ½ cups
Honey - ½ cups
Dijon Mustard - 1 tbsp.

Method

Mix altogether. You can eat this with whatever you desire.
It makes a great dipping sauce as well.

Milk Shake

Milk - enough to make thick
Vanilla - to taste
Ice cream - 2 scoops
Egg - 1 raw

Method

Add the ice cream, and the egg to a blender. Then add the vanilla. Turn on the blender on low, and start adding the milk.

Only add enough milk to your fancy, and taste. Turn onto medium until blended. The raw egg is what makes it thick.

P.S. You can add any sort of flavoring you desire.

Espresso Delight

Ice - fill the blender
Hot espresso - strong already made 1/3 cup
Coffee tranny – to taste, and whatever kind you desire

Method

Crush the ice; add the syrup, and espresso. Blend, and serve in glasses.

Sunset Orange

Ice enough to fill blender
Frozen concentrated orange juice half a can

Method

Blend and serve right away

Mar's Mac Sauce

Mayonnaise - ½ cups
French dressing - 2 tablespoons
Sweet pickle relish green - 4 teaspoons
Finely minced white onion - 1 tablespoon
White vinegar - 1 teaspoon
Sugar - 1 teaspoon
Salt - 1/8 of a teaspoon

Method

Combine all the ingredients in a bowl.

P.S. The French dressing is the magic ingredient.

Marlene made this recipe up when she was fourteen years old for a boyfriend. This was before she ever entered a *Mcdonald's.*

Barbeque Sauce

Ketchup - ½ cup
Soy sauce – 4 tbsp.
Brown sugar - 1/4 cup
Garlic spice - 1 teaspoon
Seasoning Salt – 2 teaspoons
Cajun spice – 1 tbsp.

Method

Mix altogether, and use. You do not need to cook it.

Marlena Burger

Hamburger - 1 ½ pounds
Ketchup, mustard, and mayo
Onions - Chopped fine
Buns

Make into patties, and put in a frying pan. When ten minutes has past, flip them. Put a bit of black pepper on them. Cover, and fry until done.

Add mayo on the bottom, and then lots of small chopped onions. Add a little bit of mustard, and green relish. Put the hamburger on top. Add ketchup, and lettuce.

Candied Yams

Yams - 3 cut in large size chunks
Butter - 1/4 cup
Brown sugar - 1 cup
Cinnamon - 1 tablespoon
Marshmallows - large white, 1 bag

Method

Put tin foil under the baking dish in the oven. Put yams into a pan, and add everything else. Do not add the marshmallows yet. Bake at 375F until yams are tender.

Now add a bag of large white marshmallows on top. Bake until they are nice, and gold.

P.S. This is a must for a traditional turkey Christmas dinner.

Turkey

Turkey -   any size
Water - ¼ quart
Thyme - to taste
Rosemary - to taste
Savory - to taste
Pepper - to taste
Onion - one large
Garlic powder - to taste
Chicken base - 3 tablespoons

Method

Clean the turkey, and stuff it. Put into a roast pan, and add water. Put all the spices all over the turkey.

The turkey should be covered with thyme. Cut the onion in half, and add onion to pan. Add the garlic to the water, and chicken base. Bake on 125F all night long.

In the morning uncover, and allow the top to get golden brown.

Chop Suey

Macaroni - cooked one bag
Hamburger - 2 pounds fried
Onion - one large minced
Tomatoes - 1 large can
Pepper - a dash

Method

Fry the onions with the hamburger until done. Add cooked macaroni to this. Add everything together, and cook some more. Do this on top of the stove on low. Serve with bread or fresh buns

Potato Salad

Potatoes - 1 large potato pot of mashed, and cooked
Onion - 1 medium minced
Dill pickles - 4 chopped small
Mustard - 1 tablespoon
Eggs - 6 boiled
Garlic powder - 1 teaspoon
Pepper - a few shakes
Miracle whip - enough to make it moist
Pimento - 2 teaspoons to taste if you have it
Paprika - Enough to sprinkle on top

Method

Add everything then add circles of chopped eggs on the
top. Cover with paprika, and then chill this in a fridge.

Surprise Potatoes

Hash browns any kind - 2 bags
Sour cream - one cup
Cheese - any white soft kind
Bacon bits - to add to top

Method

Mix the sour cream, and cheese into the potatoes in a pan.
Cover with bacon bits. Bake on 350F until brown.

Pot Roast Dinner

One big pork or beef roast
1 large Spanish onion - cut in large pieces
Crushed tomatoes – 1 large can
Hunts tomato sauce - 1 large can
Tomato soup - 1 can
Tomato paste - 1 can
Baby carrots - 2 small bags
Pepper - a dash
Garlic salt - to taste
Seasoning salt - to taste
Chives - a few dashes
Potatoes - 5 large cut in large chunks
Turnip - 1 cut in large chunks

Method

Add the roast to the middle of a roast pan. Add everything else to this. Roast covered in the oven on 375F for 2 hours.

Pork Tenderloin Stir Fry

Pork Tenderloin - 1 ½
Worchester sauce - to taste
Onion - 1
California style frozen vegetables - 2 cups
Oil - ¼ cup
Seasoning salt - to taste
Garlic powder - to taste
Pepper - a dash

Method

Slice the tender loin into thin slices with some of the spices. Fry in the oil a bit, and add some Worchester. Then add the onion. When this becomes translucent, add the vegetables. Also some more spices to taste.

Serve on rice

Italian Pasta Salad

English Cucumber - one unpeeled
Red onion - one sliced thin
Fussily - 3/4 of a box cooked
Mushrooms - 1 cup cut in pieces
Radish - 5 sliced peeled
Green pepper - 1 sliced in long slices
Red pepper - one sliced in long slices then cut in half
Tomatoes, fresh small cherry salad tomatoes
Mayonnaise - ½ cup
Italian salad dressing - one small bottle

Method

Mix everything altogether, and chill. If you feel you need to add a little more mayonnaise then do so.

Mars Ball Dinner

Ground beef - 2 pounds
Large egg - 1
Oatmeal - ¼ cup
Seasoning salt - to taste
Onion salt - to taste
Ketchup - one cup
Brown sugar - 1/4 cup

Method

Mix the first 5 ingredients altogether in a bowl. Make large meatballs, and put into a baking pan. Cook in oven on 400F until done. Add the brown sugar and ketchup together. Also add some seasoning salt. Mix this, and add to the meatballs. Bake for another 15 minutes.

P.S. These go very well with white rice with butter on top. Also some fresh cooked vegetables especially corn.

Coleslaw

Cabbage - ¾ of a head cut it in large chunks
Carrots - 4
Mayonnaise - enough to make it. It is hard to tell how much just keep adding a bit at a time until to your liking.
White sugar - 3 tablespoons

Method

Chop cabbage and carrots fine, and add to a bowl. I use a cheese grater or food processor. Mix everything in the bowl.

Baked Beans

Soldier beans - one bag and soak overnight covered with water.
Onion - 1 large
Molasses - 1 cup
Brown sugar - ½ cup
Ketchup - ¾ cup
Yellow mustard - 1 tablespoon
Bacon - ½ pound chopped into pieces
Garlic salt - 2 tablespoons
Some seasoning salt - 2 tablespoons

Method

Turn the oven on to 375F. Cut the onion in half. Add one of the halves to the pan. Chop the other half into pieces.

Add everything to the beans. Every half hour look at them. You might need to add more water.

Add a half cup of molasses more in the middle of cooking.

This might take five hours or so to get done.

Herbs De Provence Chicken

Chicken legs - 3
Flour - ¼ cup
Bread Crumbs - one cup
Seasoning salt - 1 teaspoon
Garlic salt - ½ teaspoon
Pepper - ½ teaspoon
Herbs de Provence - 1 1/2 teaspoon
Rosemary - ½ teaspoon

Method

Cut the thighs from the leg. You now need to clean the
thighs. Look on the back of the thigh near the bones that go
up it. If you take your thumb up that, you will find liver
like stuff. Remove all of this. Now wash all the chicken
with cold water.

Add all the other ingredients together in a plastic bag.
Add two pieces at a time, and shake the chicken in it.

Place some tin foil onto a pan, and put the chicken on it.
Put in a 400F oven. Make sure the sides of the tin foil have
a fold to it. Otherwise, the oil from the chicken will go off
it.

Turn the chicken in a half hour. Always bake chicken 45
minutes or it becomes too dry if more. If you cook it less, it
will not be done.

Biscuits

Double this recipe for more than two people.

White flour all purpose - 2 cups
Shortening - 1/3 cups
Salt - a dash
Baking Powder - 2 ½ tbsp.
Milk - ¾ cup
Butter for on top

Method

Add the flour, baking powder, and salt in a bowl. Blend the shortening in until it looks like course oatmeal. Make a well in the center, and add the milk.

Mix until it starts to come away from the bowl. Add some flour onto a board. Then put the biscuit dough onto it.

Kneed for a few minutes until soft, and roll it until 1 inch thick. Cut out circles, and add to a greased pan. Put them close together. Brush a bit of butter on the top. Bake for 15 minutes at 450F

P.S.

Try replacing a biscuit rather than an English muffin. When you are making eggs Benedict, it is good.

Texas Style Deep Fried Fish

White Fish - filleted any kind cut in medium chunks
Fish fry
Salt and pepper - to taste
Cajun spice - to taste

Method

Sprinkle some spices onto the medium size cut chunks. Dip the fish into the fish fry, and deep fry in hot clean oil. It will be done when it comes to the top of the oil. Sprinkle some more Cajun spice on them.

P.S. You don't want to overcook it or the fish will get dry.

Fluffy Pancakes

White flour - 1 ½ cups
White sugar - 2 tablespoons
Baking powder - 3 ¼ tablespoons
Salt - a dash
2 eggs
Water - ¾ cup

Method

Mix first five ingredients then stir a little. Add the water, and you can add a bit more. It should not be a really runny batter.

Put some butter in a frying pan. Do this on a little lower then medium heat. Add 1 ¼ cups of batter. Little or more, whatever size you like.

Fry on the bottom side until bubbles are on the top. Turn then allow to brown a bit on the bottom. Turn again, and fry just a bit more.

Mexican Chop Suey

Hamburg - 1 ½ pounds
Onion - 1 small diced small
Green pepper - a half of one diced medium
Taco seasoning - 1 package
Macaroni - 3 cups

Method

Fry the hamburger, onions, and green pepper. While doing
this, boil and drain macaroni. Add the taco seasoning to
the hamburger. Also add one cup of water. Then let this sit
for 10 minutes, and add to the macaroni.

Royal Potatoes and Steak

Potatoes - 6 cut in medium size cubes
Red Pepper - 1
Onions - 1
Garlic spice - a tab
Seasoning salt - 1 teaspoon
Chives - 2 tablespoons dried
Steak - 2 small of high quality
Cajun Spice - a tab

Method

Cut raw potatoes in medium size cubes about the size of a playing dice. Deep fry the cubes in hot oil. While the potatoes ate frying, put a bit of oil in a frying pan. Cut the red pepper in thin half inch slices. Cut the onion the same. Fry both just a little. Add the golden brown potatoes, and the chives. Add all the spices. Add the steak in the middle of the potatoes. Add the Cajun spice, a tab of seasoning salt. Fry on both sides to your liking.

Breakfast Eggs Benedict Pizza

Bread dough - enough to make a size to your pan
Béarnaise sauce - enough for your pizza dough
Spinach - cooked enough to thinly cover the pizza pan
Canadian bacon - enough to thinly cover the pan
Monterey jack cheese - enough to thinly cover pan
Sunnyside up fried eggs - 5
Cajun Spice - to tenderly sprinkle on top

Method

Make the bread dough, and form it in the pan. You can either make it thick crust or thin to your own liking. Butter the top of the crust, and add the béarnaise sauce.

Add a large tablespoon of dill to the béarnaise sauce. Thinly put cooked spinach all over the top of the sauce. Add the Canadian bacon thinly all over the top of the spinach. Thinly cover all this with the Monterey jack cheese.

Bake until the cheese is melted. When done, add the fried sunny side eggs on top. Serve.

Mac and Cheese

Macaroni - cooked enough to fill a casserole dish
Tomato soup - 1 can
Marble cheese - 2 cups graded
Bread crumbs - 1 cup
Butter - to dab dollops on top

Method:

Boil macaroni in boiling water with a couple tablespoons of oil. Darin and put in a bowl. Add the soup, and cheese. Put in the casserole dish. Mix ½ cup of shredded marble cheese to the bread crumbs. Put on top of the casserole. Put teaspoons of butter on top, and bake at 375 degrees. You will know when it is done when the top is golden.

Omelet

Omelets are an amazing thing. You can add anything you like in the middle. You can use any cheese you desire. They are not the easiest thing to get learn to make. I have always enjoyed making them so here is my version.

Eggs - 2 large
Milk - 3 tablespoons
Water - one teaspoon
Onions - 1 tablespoon chopped fine
Green pepper - 4 tablespoons chopped fine
Marble cheese - ½ cup shredded
Pam

Method

Mix the first three ingredients in a bowl. Add the next two, and stir. Get a small frying pan hot, and then spray it all with pam even the sides.

Add the egg mixture, and let it fill the pan. Cook on medium heat. As it is cooking, lift a little piece on the side with a spatula. Lift your pan a little so a bit of the runny egg can drip down into where you are holding up. Let the side down, and the pan. Let it cook a bit more. Then lift up a little piece of the side again, and let a little bit more of the runny run into it. Let the pan down, and keep doing it. When the top is done looking runny, add the cheese.

Lift one side right over the top of the other side
with a spatula. Let it only cook long enough to
let the cheese inside to melt.

This is enough for two people, when cut in half. I eat it
with white toast. It goes really well with asparagus on the
side to.

Mushroom Chicken

Chicken - 1 whole
Potatoes - 3 cups baby round
Carrots - 2 large cut in large chunks
Onion - 1 large cut in medium size pieces
Turnip - 1 small cut in medium size chunks
Cabbage - 1 small cut in chunks
Mushroom soup - 2 cans
Chicken Broth - ½ small can
Herbs de providence - enough to put all over top
Seasoning salt - 1 teaspoon
Garlic salt - 1 teaspoon
Thyme - 1 teaspoon

Method

Put chicken in a slow cooker. Add everything around the chicken. Add the soup, broth, and spices. On top of the chicken add the herbs de providence, and the thyme. Slow cook on low for 6 hours. It you are doing it in the oven bake on 375 until the chicken is done.

Deconstructed Chicken

How to make a deconstructed Chinese meal. Something meant to go all in one dish, and taste like barbecue chicken. Although it is made from pork chops.

Pork Chops - 2 large with fat on
Ketchup - ¾ cup
Soy Sauce - ¼ cup
Aunt Jamima syrup - ½ cup
Cajun spice - ¼ cup
Garlic salt - 3 tablespoons

Method

Put the unthawed pork chops in a through away silver pan. Pup the ketchup all over the top of both. Do the same with the soy sauce, and then the spices.

With your hands, mix the pork chops around the sauce on both sides. Bake in a hot oven on 375, until the pork chops are getting black on the edges.

Make the honey garlic noodles as the pork chops are cooking. Here is the recipe.

Ramen Noodles – 1 package any kind as you will be using the packaged seasoning. Just boil it in water, and drain.

Raman Noodles – 2 packages cooked, and drained without the seasoning
Oil – ¼ cup
Honey – quarter cup
Lemon juice – a few big squirts

Method

Add the oil to a hot frying pan, and add the noodles. Add the honey, and lemon juice. Add a tad of salt, and stir over medium heat until hot.

Boiled Eggs

Eggs - 4 to 8
Cold water - enough to full frying pan ¾ way up
Salt - a 1 tablespoon

Method

Put the cold water in the electric frying pan, and add eggs.
Let the water boil, and leave going for 10 minutes. Turn off
the pan, and let eggs sit in water for 15 minutes.

To crack open just tap the middle with a point of a knife.
Cut in half, and use a spoon to take the egg out of each half.

French Fries in Electric Frying Pan

Potatoes - 5
Shortening - 2 packages

Method

Peel potatoes, and into French-fries. Put them into cold water. Add enough shortening to the electric frying pan until
half full. Let it get hot. Add one raw French fry to the oil
buntil it starts to fry.

Dry the fries on a towel, and add them to pan, Make sure
they are not on top of each other. Fry until done. It usually
takes at least 45 minutes. Keep turning as they are frying.

When done, put some paper towel on a plate. Take the
French fries out onto this. Then lift the paper towel out
from under them. Add salt, and enjoy.

Beef Samosas

For the pastry:

1 1/2 plain flour
4 tbsp. vegetable oil
1/2 tsp salt water

For the filling: 2 large potatoes (boiled in their skin)
¾ cups of minced beef
3 tbsp. oil
1 tsp cumin seeds
1/4 tsp dried onion
A large piece of ginger, finely grated
2 green chilies, finely chopped
1 tsp ground coriander
1/2 tsp chili powder
1 tbsp. lemon juice
1 tsp toasted and ground cumin seeds
1 tsp salt (or to taste)
Generous handful of chopped coriander leaves
oil for deep frying

Method

Peel the boiled potatoes and dice them very finely. Add a little oil to a wok or frying pan and fry the cumin seeds until fragrant and aromatic. Then add the ginger and chillies and fry for 1 minute.

Add the beef and fry until nicely browned. Now add all the other ingredients (except the coriander leaves) and stir to coat the vegetables in oil.

Cook gently for 5 minutes (try not to break up the potatoes) then add the coriander leaves and stir to mix in. Take off the heat.

For the pastry, add the flour, salt and oil to a bowl. Rub with your fingers until the mixture resembles fine bread-crumbs. Add water a little at a time until the mixture comes together as a firm dough. Put onto a floured surface and knead well. Return to a bowl and allow to rest for 20 minutes before kneading once more.

Make a paste from 1 tbsp. flour and 2 tbsp. water. Mix thoroughly and set aside.

Divide the dough into 9 pieces, roll into balls and cover with a damp cloth. Place a ball on an oiled surface and roll into a 20cm circle. Cut in half with a knife and lift up. Bring the cut edges together to form a cone and seal with the flour paste you just made.

Press to form a good seal then fill the cone with 2 tbsp. of the potato and beef mixture. You should be left with about a 5mm overlap at the top which you can overlap and seal with the flour paste to close the samosa. Repeat until all the pastry and potato and beef mix is used-up, covering those samosas you've already made with a damp cloth to prevent them from drying out.

Add oil to a depth of about 5cm in a wok and bring to tem-perature on medium heat (don't make the wok too hot or the samosas will turn out soggy.

It's ready when a small piece of pastry dropped into the oil sizzles and rises to the surface. Add the samosas to the oil (don't over-crowd) and fry gently until colored golden brown. Turn once or twice (if you turn too often they have a tendency to break. Lift with a slotted spoon and drain on kitchen paper. Serve hot with a sweet and sour sauce.

SWEETS

Lemon Bread

Butter - 1½ cups
Sugar - 2 cups white
Eggs - 3
Lemon juice - from 3 lemons
Vanilla - 1 teaspoon
Lemon rind - just a little
Flour - 3 cups
Milk - 1½ cups you might not to use it all, but maybe more.
Make sure the batter is thick not drippy

Method

Mix butter, and sugar until creamy. Add the eggs and mix.
Add lemon juice, rind, vanilla, and mix. Put ½ teaspoon of
vinegar in ½ cup of the milk, and save.

Add half of the flour, and mix. Use half of the milk and
mix. Add the rest of the flour, and mix. Then, add the milk
with vinegar, and mix.

Let all of this set for a half hour, and them place in buttered
bread pans. Bake on 375F until toothpick comes out clean.

Orange Bread

Just add orange, and very small amount of rind instead of
lemon juice. You should only use a small dab of rind.

Walnut Bread

Add almond extract, and one cup of walnuts instead of
lemon. Or leave the lemon, and add the walnuts also.

Santa's Pie

Crushed graham crackers - 4 cups
Butter - ½ cup melted
White sugar - ½ cup
Chocolate chips - 1 ½ cups
Chocolate pudding - enough to fill shell

Method

Add the first three ingredients to a pan, and mix. Form into a pie shell. Put into a 400F oven, and bake for five minutes or so.

Melt chocolate chips, and add on to the shell. Put in the fridge to harden.

Make the chocolate pudding. When the chocolate is hard take out of fridge. Put pudding all on top, and add some chocolate sprinkles on.

Royal Icing

Icing sugar - 2 cups
Egg whites - 2
Cream of tartar - 1 ½ tablespoons

Method

Whip this with an electric mixer. It should be fluffy, and thick.

Cookie Thumbs

Butter - 1½ cups
Sugar - 2 cups white
Eggs - 3
Vanilla - one tablespoon
Flour - 3 ½ cups white
Milk - 2 cups more or less
Baking Soda - 2 tablespoons
Cream of tartar - 2 tablespoons

Method

Blend butter and sugar. Add eggs and blend, and then add vanilla, and stir. Add half of the flour, and stir. Add half of the milk, and stir.

Add the rest of the flour, baking soda, and cornstarch. Add the rest of the milk and stir. Use one tablespoon of Jam for each, on buttered cookie sheet. Make sure they are not close together. Have a glass of cold water nearby. Dip the finger beside your thumb in the cold water. Twirl it around a bit in the middle of each cookie.

You might need to put more water on your finger. You do for each cookie. Add your favorite jam, and bake at 350F. If the first batch is thin, add more flour to the next batch. These should puff up high. It is wise just to prepare each sheet as you bake it. Just bake until they are brown on the bottom. These cook rather fast so watch the bottom closely.

P.S. You can use this as a base for many cookies. For example, you can add chocolate chips, and nuts. Just don't put the fingerprint, and jam in the middle.

Golden Brownies

Flour - sifted one cup
Baking powder - ½ of a teaspoon
Baking soda - 1/8 teaspoon
Salt - a dash
Butter - 1/3 of a cup
Brown sugar - 1 cup
Egg - 1 and beaten
Vanilla - 1 tablespoon
Chocolate chips - ½ of a cup
Maple syrup - 3/8 of a cup
Butter - ¼ cup
Brown sugar - 3/8 of a cup
Cream cheese - softened one cup
Maple extract or flavoring - ½ of a teaspoon

Method

Sift together sifted flour, baking powder, baking soda, and salt. Mix well and set aside. Melt butter add brown sugar, and mix well. Add egg also vanilla, and blend. Add flour mixture a little at a time, mixing well. Stir in white chocolate chips, and spread into a 9" square pan. Bake at 350F 20-25 minutes. Or until tester inserted in center comes out clean. It should be slightly fudge looking.

Combine syrup and butter. Cook over low heat until butter is melted. Stir in brown sugar until dissolved. Remove from heat, and beat in cream cheese also maple extract until smooth. Heat again either over low heat or in the microwave at short intervals. You want it to reach desired sauce consistency. Serve sauce over warm brownies topped with vanilla ice cream.

Chocolate Chews No bakes

Dried chow mien Chinese noodles - one package
These can be asked for at your local grocer
Chocolate Chips - ¾ of a large bag
Icing sugar - ¾ of a cup white
Honey roasted peanuts - 1 ½ cup

Method

Melt the chocolate chips in the microwave. Stir while it is cooking, and it doesn't all need to be melted. It doesn't take long. Add the icing sugar, and the noodles. Place waxed paper on a cookie sheet. Add one oversized tablespoon of pumps on sheet. Do this until cookies are gone. Place in the fridge until cold.

Cinnamon Buns

One raw bread recipe
Brown Sugar - one large bag
Cinnamon - 2 tablespoons
Butter - One pound less ¼ melted
Icing sugar - ¾ cup

Method

Roll your raw bread dough out. Make it about one foot across, and start rolling out. It is a good idea to go a foot ahead or so. Mix all the ingredients together above. Add some all over the top of the bread. Start at one end, and start rolling it over, and over. Until you make a jelly roll. Cut this to make one-inch circles.

In a pan that has a very tall edge, add the left over from the mixture. If you have one left, you will need to make more. You need to add at least an inch of it into the bottom of the pan. Place the buns on top, and bake at 375. Take out. Make light syrup to drizzle on top of each. You can leave these in the pan. It really is a good idea to use a through away tin one. You can get them at your local grocer.

How to make the drizzle for the top

Icing sugar - one cup
Milk - only enough to make so you can drizzle it from a fork. It does not take more than a couple dabs of milk. Keep stirring, and place a fork in it. If it drizzles the way you like, it is done. Now use a fork, and drizzle the icing over the cinnamon buns.

Pecan Chocolate Peanut Butter Balls

Peanut butter - 2 cups
Butter - 4 tbsp.
Icing sugar - 1 1/2 cups
Milk - 1 tbsp.
Pecans - one cup crushed
Dates minced - ½ cup
Maraschino cherries red - 7 minced
Chocolate chips - 2 bags
Shortening - ¼ cup

Method

Mix peanut butter, and the butter together. Add icing sugar and mix. Add the milk and mix. You might need to add a bit more icing sugar if they are runny. Add everything else, but not the last two ingredients.

Make into balls, and put on tin foil. Melt the chocolate, and shortening in a microwave. It doesn't take long. Dip each ball into the chocolate, and put in fridge. I put some green, and red sprinkles on top while hot.

Candy Flan

One recipe for sugar cookies
Thick sweet milk - ¾ cup
Coconut - 1 bag
Walnuts - a hand full

Method

Put the sugar cookie mixture into a pan. Mix the milk, coconut, and walnuts together. Put this on top of the sugar
cookies mixture.

Bake in a 350F oven until done. Allow this candy flan to
cool. Put some white icing on this. Put toasted coconut on
top.

Toffee

Corn syrup - 1 pint
Brown sugar - 2 cups
Milk - ½ cup
Buttermilk powder - 2 tablespoons
Cherry juice - 3 tablespoon's
Salt - a few grains only
Mazola oil - 1 tablespoon
Vanilla - 6 drops
Nuts - a hand full of any kind

Method

Combine the ingredients except the nuts or vanilla. Boil
until the mixture forms a fairly firm ball. When tried in
cold water 252 degrees. Add a little bit to some cold water.
It should come out like toffee. If not, boil a bit longer. Add
the vanilla, and beat a few minutes.

Cook until the mixture is thick. Add the nuts on the bottom
of a greased pan. Add the toffee on to. Let stand several
hours to become firm. Cut in section's with a sharp knife,
and wrap in waxed paper

Mars Chocolate Chip Cookies

Butter - 1 cup
White sugar - 1 cup
Brown sugar - 1/4 cup
Eggs - 2
Vanilla - 2 1/2 tbsps.
White all-purpose flour - 2 1/4 cups
Baking powder - 2 ½ tbsps.
Salt - ¼ tsp
Chocolate chips - 2 cups milk chocolate

Method

Add the butter, and sugars, and mix. Add the eggs then mix. Then add the vanilla, and mix. Add the flour, baking powder, and salt then mix. Add the chocolate chips, and mix.

Grease a cookie sheet lightly, and leave space for rising. Use a teaspoon, and use quite a bit for each cookie. Bake at 350F until brown on the bottom. This should take 10 minutes or so.

Always make sure you clean the pan in cold water. Do this before making your next batch. The pan needs to be cool. Allow each batch to cool a bit on the baking sheet. Do this before removing to the cupboard to cool more.

Heavens Squares

Chocolate chips or butterscotch - one bag
Butter - ¼ pound
Peanut butter - 1 cup
Marshmallows - colored one bag

Method

Melt the first 3 ingredients. Heat and add the marshmallows. Put in pan, and keep in the fridge. Cut in squares.

Chocolate No Bakes

White sugar - 2 cups
Cocoa - ¼ cup
Canned milk - ½ cup
Oatmeal - 2 cups
Coconut - 2 cup
Peanut butter - 3 tablespoons

Method

Pour white sugar into a pot. Now add the cocoa. Add the canned milk. Let this just come to a boil for one minute. Now add the oatmeal to a bowl, and the coconut.

Take off, and add the peanut butter. Stir and add to the oatmeal, and coconut. Mix, and add a tablespoon at a time on wax paper. Allow to cool.

Santa's Fudge

Chocolate chips - 2 cups
Butter - 1/4 cups
Cherry juice - 2 tablespoons
Peanut butter - 1/4 cup
Marshmallow cream – 1/2 bottle
Coconut - 1 cup

Method

Melt the first three ingredients in a microwave or stove. Take off when melted, and add peanut butter.

Mix the coconut in, and then the marshmallow cream. When adding the cream, don't mix a lot. Put in a pan, and into the fridge.

P.S. You don't need to add the coconut.

Pumpkin Bread

Butter - 1/2 cup
Baking oil - 1 cup
Eggs - 3
White Sugar – one cup

Brown sugar - ¼ cup
Flour - 2 1/4 cups
Baking powder - 1 tablespoon
Baking soda - 2 tsp
Pumpkin - 1 ½ cups
Cinnamon - ½ tsp
Vanilla - 2 tsp

Method

Mix the butter, oil, and eggs together. Add the sugars, and mix. Add the flour, baking powder, and baking soda, and mix well. Add everything else, and mix. Grease three small bread pans. Bake on 375F. Keep checking until a tooth pick comes out clean. Usually this will take ½ hour or so.

La Crème Cake

Butter - 1 1/2 cup
Sugar - 2 cups white
Eggs - 3
White flour - 3 cups
Baking powder - 3 1/2 large tablespoons
Irish Crème or any other crème that you like

Method

Mix butter then add sugar. Mix and then add eggs. Mix
again, and then add flour, baking powder. Mix then add
enough crème to make it the right consistency. Butter pan,
and bake at 350F until toothpick comes out clean. Put
icing on top when cool.

Icing

Butter - 1 cup
Icing sugar - one bag
Flavoring - any kind
Milk to make to right consistency

Method

Mix soft butter, and start adding icing sugar. Add one cup
at a time until right thickness you desire. You might need
to add a drop of milk. You can, even, use chocolate milk
or crème.

Apple Cobbler

Apple Filling:

Tart apples - 5 cups peeled and sliced
Brown sugar - ¾ cup
Flour - 2 tablespoons
Cinnamon - 1/2 teaspoon
Salt - A dash
Butter - 1 tablespoon softened

Topping:

Flour - 1/2 cup sifted
White sugar - 1/2 cup
Baking powder - 1/2 teaspoon
Salt - 1/4 teaspoon
Butter - 2 tablespoons softened
Eggs - 2 small

Method

In a medium bowl, combine apples, 3/4 cup sugar, 2 tablespoons flour, cinnamon, 1/4 teaspoon salt, and vanilla. Put
into a buttered 9-inch square pan. Dot apples with 1 tablespoon butter.

Mix all the topping ingredients. Beat until batter is smooth.
Drop batter in 9 portions, over the apples, spacing evenly.
Batter will spread during baking.

Bake 35 to 40 minutes at 375° or until apples are tender,
and crust is golden brown. Serve warm with cream or ice
cream.

P.S. If you like extra topping, make a double batch for the
top.

Peanut Butter Fudge Candy

White Sugar - 3 cups
Milk - 1 cup
Peanut butter - 3 large tablespoons
Oreo chocolate crumbs - 3 cups
Butter - 1/3 cup
Chocolate chips - 2 cups

Method

Put the first 3 ingredients into a pan, and boil. Once it is boiling put on medium. Cook for 19 to 24 minutes. Do this until it is getting hard on the sides of the pan.

In the meantime while the fudge is cooking make the crust. Blend the Oreo's, and butter together. Butter a 9 inch pan, and add the mixture. Pat it into the pan. When the fudge is ready, pour it over the crumbs.

Allow cooling then microwave the chocolate chips. Add this on top of the fudge. Cool, and cut into squares. Cut in to pieces.

I use the same recipe for the filling for apple pie.

Lemon Pie Delight

White sugar -1 ½ cups
Egg yolks - 3
Lemon juice - from one
Water - 1 cup
Water - 2 cups hot
Cornstarch - ¼ cup

Method

Add the white sugar in the pot. Put this on a double boiler.
Add all the egg yolks in, and mix. Add the lemon juice
slowly while stirring.

Now, add the hot water, and let it boil. Make sure the water
stays boiling. Cook for about ten minutes.

Now mix the cornstarch with the cold water, and mix. Add
a bit at a time while mixing. While cooling, you can add
more cornstarch mixture if needed.

Allow this to cool, and add to a cooked pie shell. Make
some meringue, and put on top. Then bake until golden
brown on top;

Allow this to cool then serve.

Choux Pastry

1 cup water
1 stick butter
1 cup flour
1 cup eggs
1 pinch salt

Method

Put the water, and butter in a pan on top of the stove. Let the butter melt. Add the flour, and salt. Stir until the mixture comes to one side of the pan on medium heat.

Take off the stove, and start slowly adding the eggs. Mix a small amount in, and then stir. You do not want your eggs to scramble. Add the salt, and stir in well.

Put the mixture into a frosting bag. You can bake these in different sizes. You can use different baking tips on your bag. It doesn't take long to bake them on 350 degrees. Then, you can fill them with your favorite savory or dessert filling.

You can make churros from it by piping it into 6 inch strips on wax paper. Use a large round piping tip. Use at least two inches of oil hot. You will deep-fry them. Put the churros into the grease with the wax paper facing you. Put one on each small piece of wax paper. The churros will come fast off the wax paper. Remove the wax paper as soon as it comes off. Deep fry until they are light brown. They should be light in touch, and airy.

Add a cup of white sugar, and a ¼-cup of cinnamon to a brown bag. Work fast, and add churros a couple at a time to the bag. Shake, and then lay out on a plate. They are best served when made.

Orange Bread

Butter - 1 ½ cups
White sugar - 1 3/4 cups
Eggs - 3
Lemon juice - 1 tablespoon
Flour - 1 ½ cups
Baking powder - 1 tablespoon
Baking soda - 1 teaspoon
Tangerine - 1
White milk - ¼ cup
Salt - a few dashes

Method

Mix the butter in a bowl. Turn on your oven to 375. Add
the white sugar, and stir it all in. Add the lemon juice, and
stir. Add the eggs, and whip these in. Add ½ cup of the
flour, the being powder, and the baking soda. Stir this in,
and then add only the liquid from the orange, and a bit of
the milk. Stir this all together, and then add the rest of the
flour, and stir, Add a bit more milk, and then stir. Add a
dash or two of salt, and stir.

If it is the right consistency of cake put in small bread tins.
If not of cake consistency then add a little bit more milk.
You can use as large of pans as you want. It is according to
how many breads you want. It makes three if small bread
pans are used. Bake until a toothpick comes out clean.

Let it cool, and then on top drizzle the white drizzle over
the top of each cake. Put the drizzle in a plastic bottle with
a little tip at the top. It is much easier to drizzle the icing
onto the cake the way you want to.

White Drizzle

Icing sugar - 1 cup
White milk - just a little bit

Method

Start adding little drops of milk to the sugar. It wants to be the consistency not of milk, but thicker just enough that is will drizzle over the cake.

Mar's Frosty

4 cups vanilla ice cream
3 tablespoon powdered chocolate drink mix
3/4 cup milk
1 teaspoon vanilla
¼ cup cool whip

Method

Put all ingredients in a blender and mix until thoroughly combined.

To make it thinner, add more milk. For a thicker shake more like an authentic frosty use a little less milk.

Serve

Lemonade

2 cups freshly squeezed lemon juice
1/2 cup of sugar
5 cups of cold water
1 pound of fresh strawberries
1 cup of heavy cream
Fresh lemon slices
Ice

Method

Mix the lemon juice, the sugar, and 1 cup of cold water in a large pitcher.

Begin to stir until the sugar dissolves, then add the rest of your water.

Puree the strawberries with the cream and add the mixture to the lemonade.

Pour over ice

Add some fresh slices of lemon to garnish and enjoy!

Pretzels

2 cups milk
1 1/2 tablespoons (2 packets) active dry yeast
6 tablespoons brown sugar
4 tablespoons butter, melted
4 1/2 cups flour
2 teaspoons fine salt
1/3 cup baking soda
3 cups warm water
Coarse salt
8 tablespoons butter, melted in a shallow dish

Method

Warm up the milk in the microwave or on the stove for just about one and a half minutes. It should be about 110°. If it's too hot it will kill the yeast. You should be able to comfortably keep your finger in it.

Stir in the yeast and let it sit for about 3 minutes. Add the butter and sugar. Add the flour about 1 cup at a time and then add the fine salt.

Kneed for about 10 minutes with a stand mixer, or by hand. Put it in a greased bowl and cover with greased cling wrap. Let rise for 1 hour in a moist, warm place until doubled in size.

Preheat the oven to 450°. Punch down dough and divide into 12 lumps (I like to divide it in half, then divide each half into three, and then divide each remaining one in half again.

Roll them all out as thin as you can. Combine the warm water and baking soda in a wide bowl. Form the dough into pretzel shapes, then dip in the baking soda water. Place on a greased baking sheet and sprinkle with coarse salt. Bake for about 7-11 minutes or until browned. Dip each in the melted butter while hot. Serve with cheese sauce.

Cheese Sauce

3 tablespoons butter
3 tablespoons flour
3 1/2 cloves minced garlic
1 cup milk
1/8 teaspoon smoked paprika
a pinch cayenne pepper
8 oz. cheddar cheese, shredded

Method

In a saucepan, combine the butter, flour, and garlic over medium heat. Whisk until lightly browned. Whisk in the milk, paprika, and cayenne pepper and continue whisking until thickened.

Add the cheese and whisk until melted. Can be reheated in the microwave.

Marsbar's

For the chocolate nougat:

2 egg whites
¼ teaspoon cream of tartar
1½ cups sugar
1 cup light corn syrup
½ cup water
4oz melted milk chocolate
2 tablespoons cocoa powder

For the caramel:

1 cup sugar
¾ cup whipping cream
½ cup light corn syrup
4 tablespoons unsalted butter
½ teaspoon salt
½ teaspoon vanilla extract

For the chocolate:
400g of your favorite chocolate, tempered

Method

Prepare the nougat:

Grease an 8 by 8 pan and then line it with parchment paper, with excess on the sides so that you can pull it out later. Beat the egg whites with the cream of tartar to soft peaks while the sugar, corn syrup, and water cook on medium-high heat in a medium saucepan. Cook the sugar until it reaches the soft crack stage, 270°F.

Pour about a teaspoon of the sugar syrup into the egg whites and beat until incorporated. Add in another teaspoon and beat some more. Continue doing this until all the sugar syrup is incorporated. Add in the chocolate and the cocoa powder, and beat until the bowl is slightly warmer than room temperature, about three minutes. Pour into the pan.

Spread the nougat into an even layer. It might be helpful to place a piece of parchment paper on top and press down on it with your hands to do this. Let the nougat sit for ten minutes at room temperature while you prepare the caramel.

Prepare the caramel:

Cook all the ingredients together in a medium saucepan over medium-high heat until the temperature reaches 245°F, about eight minutes. Do not stir. Pour onto the nougat, and let sit for two hours.

Cut the bars:

Take out the layers by pulling on the parchment paper and then place them on a chopping board, caramel side down. Cut the bars into any size you like. Place the layers in the freezer before cutting if you're having trouble. This will be sticky.

Dip the bars:

Dip the bars using a fork in the tempered chocolate, and then let the chocolate harden at room temperature. Store the chocolate bars in the fridge, and let them sit at room temperature for twenty minutes before serving.

French Toast 40
Meat Loaf Delight 41
Egg in the Hole 42
Marinated Mushrooms 43
Honey Mustard Sauce 44
Milk Shake 45
Espresso Delight 46
Sunset Orange 46
Mar's Mac Sauce 47
Barbeque Sauce 48
Marlena Burger 49
Candied Yams 50
Turkey 51
Chop Suey 52
Potato Salad 53
Surprise Potatoes 54
Pot Roast Dinner 55
Pork Tenderloin Stir Fry 56
Italian Pasta Salad 57
Mars Ball Dinner 58
Coleslaw 59
Baked Beans 60
Herbs De Provence Chicken 61
Biscuits 62
Texas Style Deep Fried Fish 63
Fluffy Pancakes 64
Mexican Chop Suey 65
Royal Potatoes and Steak 66
Breakfast Eggs Benedict Pizza 67
Mac and Cheese 68
Omelet 69 – 70
Mushroom Chicken 71
Deconstructed Chicken 72 - 73
Boiled Eggs 74
French Fries in Electric Frying Pan 74
Beef Samosas 75 - 76
Lemon Bread 77

Made in the USA
Middletown, DE
14 May 2021